THE GREATEST RECORDS IN SPORTS
BASKETBALL'S
GREATEST RECORDS

Ryan Nagelhout

New York

Published in 2015 by The Rosen Publishing Group, Inc.
29 East 21st Street, New York, NY 10010

First Edition

Editor: Ryan Nagelhout
Book Design: Reann Nye

Photo Credits: Cover (basketball court) EKS/Shutterstock.com; cover (Thompson) Phil Walter/ Getty Images Sport/Getty Images; cover (James), pp. 5, 30 Andy Lyons/Getty Images Sport/Getty Images; p. 7 WEN ROBERTS/AFP/Getty Images; p. 9 Focus On Sport/Contributor/Getty Images; p. 11 GEORGE FREY/AFP/Getty Images; p. 12 Dick Raphael/Sports Illustrated/Getty Images; p. 13 Domenic Grant/Shutterstock.com; p.15 CRAIG LASSIG/AFP/Getty Images; p. 17 John Gichigi/ Getty Images Sport/Getty Images; p. 19 Joel Shawn/Shutterstock.com; p. 20 JEFF HAYNES/AFP/ Getty Images; p. 21 Debby Wong/Shutterstock.com; p. 23 B Bennett/Getty Images Sport/Getty Images; p. 25 Jonathan Daniel/Getty Images Sport/Getty Images; p. 27 Manny Millan/Sports Illustrated/ Getty Images; p. 29 Christian Petersen/Getty Images Sport/Getty Images.

Library of Congress Cataloging-in-Publication Data

Nagelhout, Ryan.
 Basketball's greatest records / Ryan Nagelhout.
     pages cm. — (The Greatest Records in Sports)
 Includes index.
 ISBN 978-1-4994-0232-2 (pbk.)
 ISBN 978-1-4994-0183-7 (6 pack)
 ISBN 978-1-4994-0220-9 (library binding)
 1. Basketball—Records—United States—Juvenile literature. I. Title.
 GV885.55.N34 2015
 796.323—dc23
                              2014035858

Manufactured in the United States of America

CPSIA Compliance Information: Batch #CW15PK: For Further Information contact Rosen Publishing, New York, New York at 1-800-237-9932

CONTENTS

STATS TELL THE STORY

Basketball games are full of numbers. Teams often score more than 100 points in a **professional** basketball game. Some of the best players make putting the ball through the basket look easy. Many different **statistics**, or stats, are recorded to measure different things about the game.

The National Basketball Association (NBA) is the highest men's professional basketball league in North America. It competed with the American Basketball Association (ABA) from 1967 until the two leagues merged, or combined, in 1976. Most of the records in this book will be from the NBA, but many great players called the ABA home in the 1960s and 1970s. The Women's National Basketball Association (WNBA) is where some of the best women's basketball players in the world play.

We can learn a lot about the best basketball players, such as LeBron James, by looking at their stats.

SCORING STATS

Basketball players score points by putting the ball through the basket. There are two ways to score: field goals and free throws. Field goals are shots taken from the field, or anywhere on the court. They're worth two points unless the shot is taken beyond the three-point line, which makes it worth three points. Free throws are worth one point and are taken after a foul by the other team. One player gets a shot from a line that's 15 feet (4.6 m) from the backboard, which is the back part of the basket that holds the net.

The highest-scoring NBA game ever happened on December 13, 1983, when the Detroit Pistons beat the Denver Nuggets, 186–184. Wilt Chamberlain, who played from 1959–1973, has many NBA points records, including most points in a game (100) and most points in a season (4,029).

SUPERIOR STATS
MOST POINTS IN AN NBA GAME

PLAYER	DATE	POINTS
WILT CHAMBERLAIN	3/2/1962	100
KOBE BRYANT*	1/22/2006	81
WILT CHAMBERLAIN	12/8/1961	78
WILT CHAMBERLAIN	1/13/1962	73
WILT CHAMBERLAIN	11/16/1962	73
DAVID THOMPSON	4/9/1978	73

* = active player

Wilt Chamberlain's nickname was "Wilt the Stilt" because he was taller than most other NBA players during his professional career.

Wilt Chamberlain

WILT CHAMBERLAIN
(1936–1999)

The greatest scorer in NBA history was born in Philadelphia, Pennsylvania, in 1936. Wilt Chamberlain set many NBA records, including the highest average points per game in a season, with 50.4 points per game in the 1961–1962 season. Chamberlain was **inducted** into the Pro Basketball Hall of Fame in 1979.

Good basketball players score many points over a long career. The NBA record for most points in a career is held by Los Angeles Lakers great Kareem Abdul-Jabbar, who scored 38,387 points over his 20-year career.

Michael Jordan was one of the greatest scorers in NBA history. Jordan holds the NBA record for career average points per game, with 30.12 points. He led the league in scoring 11 times in his career and led in points per game 10 times. Both of these are NBA records.

The Denver Nuggets have the highest-ever team average for points per game in a season. They scored an average of 126.5 points per game during the 1981–1982 season.

SUPERIOR STATS
CAREER NBA POINTS

PLAYER	POINTS
KAREEM ABDUL-JABBAR	38,387
KARL MALONE	36,928
MICHAEL JORDAN	32,292
KOBE BRYANT*	31,700
WILT CHAMBERLAIN	31,419

* = active player

Kareem Abdul-Jabbar

Abdul-Jabbar's most famous shot was a one-handed jump shot called the "skyhook."

KAREEM ABDUL-JABBAR
(1947–)

Born Ferdinand Lewis Alcindor Jr., Kareem Abdul-Jabbar was the first overall pick in the 1969 NBA **Draft** by the Milwaukee Bucks. He was named the league's Most Valuable Player (MVP) six times and won six NBA championships. He was inducted into the Pro Basketball Hall of Fame in 1995.

9

Great scorers can't beat the other team's five players on their own. They need good teammates to pass the ball to them. When a player passes the ball to a teammate who then scores, the passer gets credit for an assist. Point guards, who usually run the offense when a team is trying to score, often get a lot of assists.

The all-time leader in assists is John Stockton, who played for the Utah Jazz. Stockton has many assist records, including most assists in a season, with 1,164 passes that led to baskets in the 1990–1991 season.

Stockton also has some of the highest assist totals for a single game in league history. However, Scott Skiles has the all-time record, with 30 assists in a game for the Orlando Magic in 1990.

SUPERIOR STATS
CAREER NBA ASSISTS

PLAYER	ASSISTS
JOHN STOCKTON	15,806
JASON KIDD	12,091
STEVE NASH*	10,335
MARK JACKSON	10,334
MAGIC JOHNSON	10,141

* = active player

A basketball player has to quickly see when their teammates are open. Then, they can pass the ball without the other team stealing it.

John Stockton

JOHN STOCKTON
(1962–)

John Stockton was taken by the Utah Jazz as the 16th overall pick in the 1984 NBA Draft. He has the top four spots on the list for most assists in one season. Stockton led the league in assists for nine straight seasons, from 1987 to 1996, and was inducted into the Pro Basketball Hall of Fame in 2009.

ON THE REBOUND

A rebound is a stat that tracks which player picks up a loose ball after a missed shot. An offensive rebound is when a player picks up the ball after a teammate misses the basket. Defensive rebounds occur when a player picks up a loose ball after someone from the other team attempts a field goal. Total rebounds combine both offensive and defensive rebounds.

Players who get many rebounds are commonly tall and have long arms. The career leader in total rebounds is Wilt Chamberlain. He also has the top seven single-season rebound totals. Bill Russell has the next five spots on the list. Chamberlain also has the NBA record for most rebounds in a single game (55).

BILL RUSSELL
(1934–)

Bill Russell played his entire career for the Boston Celtics. He won 11 NBA championships in just 13 seasons, which is more than any other player in the league's history. Russell was inducted into the Pro Basketball Hall of Fame in 1975.

Centers are often the best players at getting rebounds. Players at this position, including Russell, have always been among the tallest players on their team.

SUPERIOR STATS
MOST CAREER TOTAL REBOUNDS IN NBA HISTORY

PLAYER	TOTAL REBOUNDS
WILT CHAMBERLAIN	23,924
BILL RUSSELL	21,620
KAREEM ABDUL-JABBAR	17,440
ELVIN HAYES	16,279
MOSES MALONE	16,212

Offensive rebounds are important because they give a team another chance to score after a missed shot. They can also give a team a fresh 24-second **shot clock** if the shot touched the rim of the basket. A defensive rebound gives possession of the ball to the team that was **defending** the basket.

Offensive and defensive rebounds were not counted separately in the NBA until the 1973–1974 season. Moses Malone has the most offensive rebounds in NBA history (6,731). He also has the most offensive rebounds in a season, with 587 in 1978–1979.

SUPERIOR STATS
MOST OFFENSIVE REBOUNDS IN NBA HISTORY

PLAYER	REBOUNDS
MOSES MALONE	6,731
ROBERT PARISH	4,598
BUCK WILLIAMS	4,526
DENNIS RODMAN	4,329
CHARLES BARKLEY	4,260

Karl Malone's record for most career defensive rebounds could be broken by current NBA stars, such as Kevin Garnett and Tim Duncan.

Karl Malone has the career record for most defensive rebounds, with 11,406. Kareem Abdul-Jabbar holds the NBA record for most defensive rebounds in a season. He had 1,111 rebounds during the 1975–1976 season.

KARL MALONE
(1963–)

Karl Malone was drafted by the Utah Jazz in 1985. He's a two-time NBA MVP and is second all-time in career NBA points. He also has the NBA record for most free throws made (9,787) and free throw attempts (13,188). Malone was inducted into the Pro Basketball Hall of Fame in 2010.

THE ART OF THE STEAL

When you're playing defense in basketball, you want to stop the other team from scoring. The best way to do that is to take the ball from them. When a player takes the ball from someone on the other team, it's called a steal.

John Stockton has the career record for most steals in NBA history, with 3,265. The NBA record for most steals in a season is held by Alvin Robertson, who had 301 steals with the San Antonio Spurs during the 1985–1986 season. The record for most steals in a game was set by Kendall Gill of the New Jersey Nets. He had 11 steals against the Miami Heat on April 3, 1999.

SUPERIOR STATS
CAREER NBA STEALS

PLAYER	STEALS
JOHN STOCKTON	3,265
JASON KIDD	2,684
MICHAEL JORDAN	2,514
GARY PAYTON	2,445
MAURICE CHEEKS	2,310

Michael Jordan was inducted into the Pro Basketball Hall of Fame in 2009. He's one of the most famous athletes in the history of American sports.

MICHAEL JORDAN
(1963–)

Michael Jordan is considered by many to be the greatest basketball player of all time. He won six NBA championships with the Chicago Bulls and led the league in points 11 times in his career. Jordan was also a skilled defensive player, ranking third on the all-time NBA steals list.

SHOOTING FOR THREE

The three-point field goal was added to the NBA rule book for the 1979–1980 season. The three-point shot has changed the way teams play defense and has led to many exciting comebacks in games.

Ray Allen has the most three-point field goals in NBA history. By the end of the 2013–2014 season, he had made 2,973 three-point shots. Point guard Stephen Curry has the record for most three-point field goals in a season. He made 272 of them with the Golden State Warriors during the 2012–2013 season. George McCloud holds the record for most three-point attempts in a season, trying for 678 three-pointers with the Dallas Mavericks in the 1995–1996 season.

RAY ALLEN
(1975–)

Ray Allen holds the NBA record for most career three-point field goals. He has also led the league in three-pointers made in a season three times in his career. He has won two NBA championships, and until 2013, he also held the NBA record for most three-pointers in a season.

Records for three-point shooting keep changing as players get better and better at this part of the game of basketball.

SUPERIOR STATS
MOST THREE-POINT FIELD GOALS IN AN NBA SEASON

PLAYER	SEASON	THREE-POINT FIELD GOALS MADE
STEPHEN CURRY*	2012–2013	272
RAY ALLEN*	2005–2006	269
DENNIS SCOTT	1995–1996	267
STEPHEN CURRY*	2013–2014	261
GEORGE MCCLOUD	1995–1996	257

* = active player

THE BIG BLOCK

Being tall in the NBA helps you score, and it also helps you play good defense. Blocking an **opponent's** shot is the best way to keep them from scoring. Some of the greatest defensive players in NBA history were tall players with long arms who could jump high into the air. This made them very successful at blocking shots.

Hakeem Olajuwon is the all-time leader in career blocks, with 3,830 in his 18-year career. Utah Jazz center Mark Eaton holds the record for blocks in a season. He blocked 456 shots during the 1984–1985 season. Eaton also holds the records for highest average blocks per game in a season (5.56 in 1984–1985) and in a career (3.5).

HAKEEM OLAJUWON
(1963–)

Born in Lagos, Nigeria, Hakeem Olajuwon was the first overall pick of the Houston Rockets in the 1984 NBA Draft. Olajuwon holds the NBA record for most career blocks. He won back-to-back NBA championships with the Rockets. Olajuwon was inducted into the Pro Basketball Hall of Fame in 2008.

A big block can make a huge difference in a basketball game!

SUPERIOR STATS
MOST CAREER BLOCKS IN NBA HISTORY

PLAYER	BLOCKS
HAKEEM OLAJUWON	3,830
DIKEMBE MUTOMBO	3,289
KAREEM ABDUL-JABBAR	3,189
MARK EATON	3,064
DAVID ROBINSON	2,954

The NBA first recorded blocks as a statistic in the 1973–1974 season. Los Angeles Lakers center Elmore Smith set the single-game record for blocks that season. He blocked 17 shots on October 28, 1973, in a win over the Portland Trailblazers. Shaquille O'Neal and Manute Bol each have recorded 15 blocks in a game, which is tied for second on the list.

Dikembe Mutombo led the NBA in blocks for five straight seasons from 1993 to 1998. That's a league record. Serge Ibaka is a current NBA player who has led the league in blocks for four years in a row as of the 2013–2014 season.

SUPERIOR STATS
MOST BLOCKS IN AN NBA SEASON

PLAYER	SEASON	BLOCKS
MARK EATON	1984–1985	456
MANUTE BOL	1985–1986	397
ELMORE SMITH	1973–1974	393
HAKEEM OLAJUWON	1989–1990	376
MARK EATON	1985–1986	369

Marcus Camby, Kareem Abdul-Jabbar, and Mark Eaton have led the NBA in average blocks per game four times. That's also a league record.

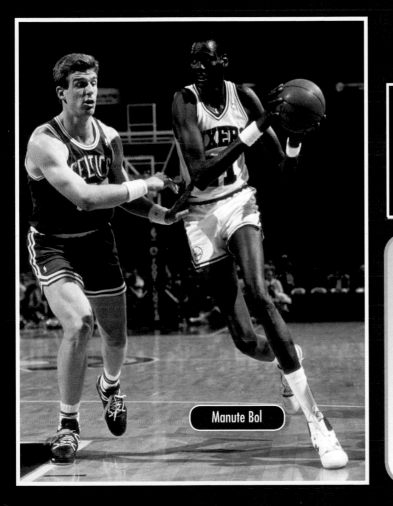

Manute Bol

During the 1987–1988 season, Manute Bol played on the Washington Bullets with Muggsy Bogues, who is 5 feet 3 inches (1.6 m) tall. The tallest and shortest players in NBA history were on the same team!

MANUTE BOL
(1962–2010)
Born in Sudan, Manute Bol was drafted 31st overall by the Washington Bullets in the 1985 NBA Draft. At 7 feet 7 inches (2.31 m) tall, Bol shares the record of tallest player in NBA history with Gheorghe Muresan.

It's easy to tell if someone played well in a basketball game when you put the different stats they recorded together. One way to do this is to count "doubles." A double is when a player gets a double-digit number (10 or more) in one of the major stat **categories**—points, rebounds, assists, steals, and blocks—in a single game. Getting two doubles is called a "double-double," and three is a "triple-double."

Oscar Robertson has the NBA record for most career triple-doubles, with 181. Wilt Chamberlain recorded the most double-doubles in NBA history—966. Magic Johnson holds the record for most career **playoff** triple-doubles. He recorded 30 triple-doubles in 190 playoff games with the Los Angeles Lakers.

OSCAR ROBERTSON
(1938–)

Oscar Robertson was drafted by the Cincinnati Royals in 1960. He was a point guard who played 10 seasons with the Royals and four with the Milwaukee Bucks, leading the NBA in assists six times. He was inducted into the Pro Basketball Hall of Fame in 1980.

LeBron James

SUPERIOR STATS
CAREER NBA
TRIPLE-DOUBLES

PLAYER	TRIPLE-DOUBLES
OSCAR ROBERTSON	181
MAGIC JOHNSON	138
JASON KIDD	107
WILT CHAMBERLAIN	78
LARRY BIRD	59

LeBron James is one of the most famous basketball players in the world. He's second on the list of career playoff triple-doubles. James could break Johnson's record someday if he continues to have success in the playoffs.

The greatest accomplishment in sports is winning a championship. NBA teams work hard all season to make the playoffs. Then, the two best teams battle for the Larry O'Brien **Trophy** in the NBA Finals. Some of the greatest players in NBA history hold playoff and championship records. These record holders could change every year as new teams and players fight for a championship.

The playoff MVP **award** is named after Bill Russell. Michael Jordan won this award all six times he made the finals. Jordan has the record for most points per game in the playoffs. He scored an average of 33.45 points per playoff game. The Boston Celtics and Los Angeles Lakers have met in the NBA Finals 12 times, which is more than any other pair of teams.

LARRY BIRD AND MAGIC JOHNSON
(1956–)   (1959–)

Larry Bird of the Boston Celtics and Magic Johnson of the Los Angeles Lakers had one of the best rivalries in NBA history. The two stars led their teams against one another in the NBA Finals three times between 1984 and 1987, with the Lakers winning two times.

Larry Bird

Magic Johnson

SUPERIOR STATS
TEAMS WITH THE MOST
NBA CHAMPIONSHIPS
(AS OF 2013–2014 SEASON)

TEAM	NBA CHAMPIONSHIPS
BOSTON CELTICS	17
LOS ANGELES LAKERS	16
CHICAGO BULLS	6
SAN ANTONIO SPURS	5
DETROIT PISTONS	3
GOLDEN STATE WARRIORS	3
MIAMI HEAT	3
PHILADELPHIA 76ERS	3

Larry Bird and Magic Johnson started their rivalry while they were in college. Their rivalry turned into a friendship they still have today.

WOMEN ON THE COURT

The WNBA started in 1997 with eight teams around the United States. The league now has 12 teams and has featured a number of stars. One of these stars, Cynthia Cooper of the Houston Comets, led the league in scoring in its first three seasons. The Comets won the first four WNBA titles, with Cooper winning MVP honors for all four of those WNBA Finals. Cooper retired in 2003, averaging 21 points per game, which is the highest in WNBA history.

Diana Taurasi has led the WNBA in scoring a record five times, as of the end of the 2014 season. Taurasi, who was a college basketball star at the University of Connecticut, has played in the WNBA since 2004. She currently sits second in career points behind Tina Thompson. Taurasi could break Thompson's record in the future because she's still an active player.

SUPERIOR STATS
CAREER WNBA POINTS

PLAYER	POINTS
TINA THOMPSON	7,488
DIANA TAURASI*	6,722
TAMIKA CATCHINGS*	6,554
KATIE SMITH	6,452
LISA LESLIE	6,263

* = active player

Diana Taurasi

Tina Thompson

The WNBA's most famous record holders continue to inspire the future stars of women's basketball.

TINA THOMPSON
(1975–)

Tina Thompson was the first ever WNBA draft pick, taken first overall by the Houston Comets in the 1997 WNBA Draft. She led the Comets to four WNBA championships along with her teammates Sheryl Swoopes and Cynthia Cooper. Thompson retired from the WNBA in 2013 as the league's all-time leading scorer.

STUDYING STATS

The way we measure the game of basketball is always changing. New stats help us keep track of different parts of the game, such as defense and three-point shooting. There are always more statistics to learn about the NBA, the WNBA, and the players who hold the sport's greatest records. Jump into the record books for yourself and see what you can find out about your favorite team or player!

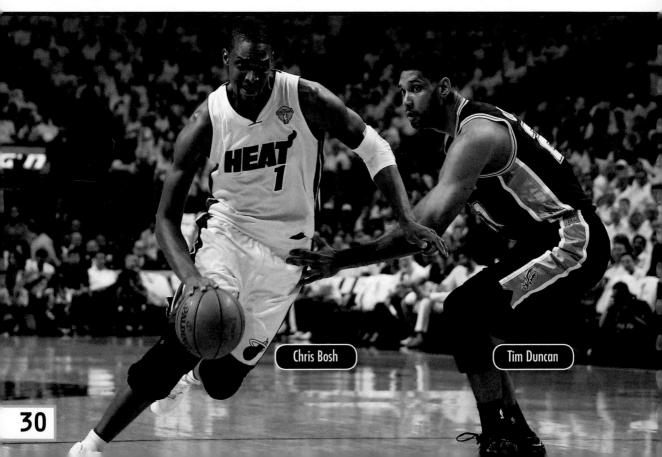

Chris Bosh

Tim Duncan

GLOSSARY

award: A prize given for doing something well.

category: A group of things that are similar in some way.

defend: To keep players on the other team from scoring.

draft: To select a player from a pool of potential players entering a sports league. Also, the process of selecting new players.

induct: To admit or bring in as a member.

opponent: The person or team you must beat to win a game.

playoff: The games played after the regular season to determine which teams will play for a sport's championship.

professional: Having to do with a job someone does for a living.

shot clock: A clock that counts down in a basketball game and limits the amount of time a team has to take a shot at the basket.

statistic: A number that stands for a piece of information.

trophy: An object given to honor an accomplishment.

INDEX

WEBSITES

Due to the changing nature of Internet links, PowerKids Press has developed an online list of websites related to the subject of this book. This site is updated regularly. Please use this link to access the list: www.powerkidslinks.com/gris/bball